AF805273

LORRAINE MARINER was born and raised in London, where she works as a librarian at the National Poetry Library in the Southbank Centre. She has published two previous collections with Picador: *Furniture* (2009), shortlisted for the Forward Prize for Best First Collection and the Seamus Heaney Centre Poetry Prize, and *There Will Be No More Nonsense* (2014).

Also by Lorraine Mariner

There Will Be No More Nonsense

Furniture

Lorraine Mariner

Little Anchors

PICADOR

First published 2026 by Picador
an imprint of Pan Macmillan
The Smithson, 6 Briset Street, London EC1M 5NR
EU representative: Macmillan Publishers Ireland Ltd, 1st Floor,
The Liffey Trust Centre, 117–126 Sheriff Street Upper,
Dublin 1 D01 YC43
Associated companies throughout the world

ISBN 978-1-0374-1171-7

Copyright © Lorraine Mariner 2026

The right of Lorraine Mariner to be identified as the
author of this work has been asserted in accordance with
the Copyright, Designs and Patents Act 1988.

All rights reserved. No part of this publication may be reproduced,
stored in a retrieval system, or transmitted, in any form, or by any means
(including, without limitation, electronic, mechanical, photocopying, recording
or otherwise) without the prior written permission of the publisher.

Pan Macmillan does not have any control over, or any responsibility for,
any author or third-party websites (including, without limitation, URLs,
emails and QR codes) referred to in or on this book.

1 3 5 7 9 8 6 4 2

A CIP catalogue record for this book is available from the British Library.

Printed and bound in the UK using 100% Renewable Electricity by Short Run Press Ltd

FSC
www.fsc.org
MIX
Paper | Supporting
responsible forestry
FSC® C116313

This book is sold subject to the condition that it shall not, by way of trade or otherwise,
be lent, hired out, or otherwise circulated without the publisher's prior consent in any form
of binding or cover other than that in which it is published and without a similar condition
including this condition being imposed on the subsequent purchaser. The publisher does not
authorize the use or reproduction of any part of this book in any manner for the purpose of
training artificial intelligence technologies or systems. The publisher expressly reserves
this book from the Text and Data Mining exception in accordance with Article 4(3)
of the European Union Digital Single Market Directive 2019/790.

Visit **www.picador.com** to read more about all our books and to buy them.

For Sofia, Elliot, Kostas and Jess

Contents

Little Anchors

The Quintessential English Family at Sunday Lunch

My true name is locked
in a silver metal box
of important family documents.
To find out that I am
the grandchild of immigrants
a key must be turned.

*

Father, the way you celebrated
our new name, the monogrammed
cutlery, the coat of arms
on a wall-mounted plaque,
did not sit easily as we got older.
Along with the Old Charm
oak dining table and Constable place mats,
I see now that you were dressing a set.

*

Father, I know that telephones
were put down on you
when you enquired after jobs,
that you and your brother
had to adopt English surnames
to get a foot in any door
but I started work in a time

of test cases and employment law.
At a great London institution
I had to show my birth certificate
to an HR assistant from your father's country
and I was ashamed, though she liked
the translation you had chosen.

*

Sometimes I meet people
whose name is my pretend name
and I hate having to explain
that I'm no relation.
Or to an Ipswich supporter
that I am not the daughter
of the footballer, or to that Mozart fan
I had no connection to the conductor.
But what is worse is knowing
that my true relations
will never be able to find me.

*

My sister has fallen in love
with a man who has given
her back her heritage.
She will take his name.
I hold on to her wedding veil
and go along for the ride.

*

Father, it was a week
after what would have been
your seventieth birthday.
They named it Brexit
as if they were launching
a chocolate bar.
For the first time
I did not regret my false name.
Your deed poll
felt like protection.

*

My true name is locked
in a silver metal box
in my parents' house,
in a suburb that voted *Leave*,
that might as well be
the bottom of the ocean.
My father understood
its treasure would never
be wanted there.

*

My sister is getting used
to people misspelling Sofia,
her daughter's name,
ph instead of an f.
I build a tower
of rainbow-coloured stacking cups
for my niece to live in
but she thinks she will never
have need of it,
knocks it down and laughs.

*

Once I had a name
that was difficult
for other people to spell
and almost impossible
for them to say.
My Irish grandmother,
who married the name,
taught me how to spell it.
And when people did try
and speak it, what they said was
Foreigner.

*

My oldest friend
remembers the name
I had until I was four
and she asks me to say it
for her and we marvel
at its combination of letters
which means it can withstand
temperatures unknown on this island
and if it's pronounced properly
it sounds like a wave of Aegean sea
coming in, going out.

When You Meet Your Second Cousin

When you meet your second cousin
for the first time and he drives
one hundred miles to collect you
from the airport and you sense

it would be wrong to offer to pay
for petrol, the car parking ticket
or the tunnel toll, do not for a moment
feel guilty. He is not collecting you.

He is collecting your grandmother –
his aunt, his mother's youngest sister –
or any one of his sisters moved to London
who will never again make this journey.

Ideal for the Tarbert Ferry

Breakfasting at Dillane's Farmhouse B&B
I watch a fellow tourist
pause at the window
weighing up the weather

and it strikes me, over twenty-five years,
how many other guests
have looked down through that glass
towards the Shannon Estuary

Mamie's cottage –
my grandma's birthplace –
my people's square of land,
part of the moistening vista

My Grandma Leaves the Orphanage at Glin

Your first period has arrived and now it's time
to leave the convent and the orphans
of the Spanish Influenza. Goodbye nuns.
Goodbye your own bed. Goodbye education

and training in domestic duties for servitude
in a class system that is unravelling.
You have a doll in a box gifted to you
one Christmas, and a poem, about a poem

being no match for a tree, memorised
to recite to your grandchildren. Your parents
and the baby are almost ten years dead
but you're not truly an orphan.

Is that one of your brothers come to collect you
in a horse and cart? Or a sister on foot
to walk you and your doll the four miles
back to Doonard along the Shannon?

I felt pity stepping into the two-room cottage
where my great-grandparents attempted
to raise ten children. But here you are
aged twelve crossing the threshold – your home

maintained by your eldest siblings Tom, John,
Maimie and Pat since they were teenagers
for Jim, Katie, Mick, Nell and you the youngest, Peggy –
and it strikes me as the finest place on earth.

My Uncle Slept in a Drawer

It was World War II
and there was no chance
of a crib so my newborn
uncle slept in a drawer.

My grandma's first baby
ended up with her childless
married sister. Her second
was given to The Church

and put up for adoption,
but this time my grandma
had a husband and she got
to keep her third baby.

Should anybody come
for him she just had to
place that drawer back into
its cabinet and slide.

Mirror Mirror

Zadie Smith imposes 15-minute mirror time limit on her daughter
HuffPost

From the age of 7
at every opportunity
I would lock myself
in my parents' bathroom
and place the lid down
on the toilet
stand on it
and stare at myself
in the mirror
for well over
15 minutes.
I loved what
I saw there.
I was Whitney and Madonna
I was accepting Grammies
I was kissing an Oscar
I was in a beige swivel chair
telling Terry Wogan
about my latest novel
I was striding purposefully
towards the door of No.10
I was bending my head
so they could drape gold medals
around my neck for every sport
that had ever been invented
depending on the season.
The mirror was a television
and I was on it
bursting with pride
fighting back
tears of joy
thanking my mother.

Ten

As 1984 turns to 1985,
secondary school is looming
and Radio 1 is full of sex.
Come the summer
I'll have a Wham! poster
on the slanted ceiling
above my top bunk
and two double-page spreads
in my scrapbook
devoted to Madonna.
Right now, in the depths
of winter, the predictable
singing of Christmas hymns
has not prepared me
for Madonna's breakout hit
and my mother is explaining
what a virgin actually is,
hot on the heels of her faltering
answer to my question of what
is so very wrong with 'Relax'
by Frankie Goes to Hollywood?
Her explanation had something
to do with my older brother
and the changes currently
occurring in his body.
Much as I adore
George Michael's hair,

the fact that we both have
hidden Greek names,
and the entire tragic narrative
on a dancefloor 'Careless Whisper'
which has set my poet's heart
aflame, I spend my pocket money
on 'We All Stand Together'
by my mother's first love,
ex-Beatle Paul McCartney,
and his rousing chorus
for cartoon frogs.

My Father's Soldiers

I never paid attention to my father's toy soldiers
until I brought a boy home and saw his reaction
to the armies lined up in their glass-fronted cabinets.
I'd meant to ask my dad some interested questions:
which was his first regiment, which ones
had he painted, which were the rarest in terms of value
(I understood about money and male teenagers).
I never got around to it and am only remembering

fifteen years later, now my father's in intensive care.
When the consultant said it was touch-and-go, I tried
to imagine death; it was my uncle (who collects the opposition)
packing the soldiers back into their boxes, an advert
for an auction in 'Military Modelling', and my mother crying
over her husband's children, who have no idea which little men
to keep for mementoes. I am inspecting the troops
while there is still touch, and this miniature Empire stays.

Could it be these ones in blue tailcoats lighting cannons
that are his favourites? Or these on horseback
with plumed hats and drawn swords? Or these, Greek
like his own father, in white pleated skirts?
Their stoic faces try to persuade me that he loves them all
equally, but at night, next door in my childhood bedroom,
some of them call out to me *Where is our captain?*
I hear their tiny feet marching, marking time.

A Year Today

I'm studying a sapling in Kensington Gardens.
Father, this is to be your tree and though we would never
have found it without the map from the Royal Parks
Adopt a Tree, already I've a sense of familiarity.

Close to Soldiers Walk, you can see the Round Pond
where you and your brothers sailed toy boats,
not far from where my mother bowled to an oak,
you batted with your black City Gent umbrella.

Later we will walk to the street where you grew up,
not the house, that would be too much,
but Aphrodite's Taverna to toast Greece your team's victory –
Dad, we supported them so well they've won the cup.

I worried about where my love for you would go.
Eating stuffed vine leaves I think I know it's in the trees,
in the wood that makes a coffin, a ship, a set of goal posts,
in an ash we hope will grow high as a cathedral,

high as a long ball soaring above the Portuguese turf,
kicked by a hero before a sea of blue and white shirts.

The Glass Jail

He fell
He falls (Tenses are everywhere.)
Deep down into a glass jail.
W. S. GRAHAM

On Saturday afternoons in winter she goes back there.
Her father getting drunk in front of the football.
The scores all in now, he plays his sad songs
on repeat, drinking, disappearing into the vinyl
where he cannot be reached. Her mother has not listened
to the record player since her husband's death.
All these years their daughter assumed it was broken.

It is not appropriate to talk about her drunk father.
She tries it from time to time and the words
come out like the dimples on a beer glass –
magnified speech bubbles, giant clumsy teardrops.
Workaholic (you will only be shaming your father)
alcoholic (you will only be shaming yourself).
She writes it in the third person, makes it plural:

He loved drink more than he loved his children.

Most people assume that he died of cancer.
She does not put them right. Her father scratched
all his favourite records; no matter.
She has learned the lyrics by heart. The glass tankard
rests in her chest, she keeps her drunk father there,
blurred and distorted. The glass tankard rests.

Run Away to Sea

I half believed it could be true,
the dream my father did not die.
He'd left to join a freighter's crew;
waking, I half believed it true.
There'd be a quayside rendezvous,
once more I'd look him in the eye.
All day I half believed it true,
the dream my father did not die.

Hands Face Space

they said
    no poems
        about Handwashing

but Elliot
    my hands
        were raw

and I couldn't travel
    to where you were
        sleeping

and hold you
    for the first time

people's memories
    can be very short
        and I want
            to remember

it all seems so long ago
    and yet
        your hand
            still disappears

inside mine

Purl

Having mastered purl,
thanks to my mother's patience,

I think of her mother
who could knit anything

and imagine my ancestors'
needles by the fire.

In a time of plague
I've been feeling medieval.

In and around and off,
over and over.

A pouch for my mother's iPhone,
mittens and a cap for the baby.

Protection.
Protection.

I Couldn't Write and Took to Embroidery

My life had become affluent Victorian lady,
trapped alone in a room with daily turns
in the park, so why not fully embrace it?

I stitched my absent beloved *Happy Birthday*
in tiny kisses alongside his dream helicopter.
My sister's engagement got a lyric inspired

by Beyoncé, *He put a ring on it*, though the bling
I sewed in yellow and grey thread was no match
for what now adorned her third finger.

I fashioned and sent anyone who had treated me
with kindness a decoration to hang
on their Christmas tree. I waited for release,

for words to return, but in the meantime
I felt the power in the needle setting down
my nephew's name and the date he arrived safely.

Some Books Draw Water Towards Them

Just like my collected W. S. Graham
took the worst of my foolish decision
to keep houseplants on top of the bookcase
holding the titles I treasure most

and the way an anthology of river poetry
happened to be in my rucksack
when I got caught in a week's worth
of rain falling in fifteen minutes,
the tidelined pages seeming to be the state
for which the poems had been longing,

it's only proper, as summer turns to autumn,
that this notebook, which got soaked
by a bedside glass, is where I write
warped words now that tears come

I Built Myself a House of Books

I wake, call today's colour russet, the red brick
of my parents' house, my dad's faux-leather-bound books.

Can't face Rightmove again, instead I construct
a wall of words, a poem to publish in a book.

I play around with titles, I'm a town planner choosing
street names, poems gather into an address book.

Buildings are rising across the river. No bricks,
glass and cladding for people who don't own books.

Can they be trusted? Three times my salary might buy
a garage. There's no money in lending books.

Don't think about that call from the mortgage broker.
I'll bring boxes home from the library, pack up my books.

Maybe it's time to let go of the brick-sized collecteds.
I'll be hard-nosed as an estate agent, part with some books.

The unread novels given as gifts, the ones signed to me
from poets but my heart's not touched by their book.

I no longer qualify for a twenty-five-year loan,
do I even have time to reread this many books?

I come across the phrase 'lazy architects' in a poem
and know it to be true, recall that viewing I booked

last week, a bedroom overlooking the Thames, a bed
but no space to store my clothes or books.

I won't let today turn the colour of a breeze block.
Maybe I could fit some corner shelves for my books?

Sometimes I Kept Things

Sometimes I kept things
that people left at the library
where I work. Sunglasses,

a kitten purse for my niece
containing a plastic coin,
another woman's husband.

I gave their owners
a few months
to reclaim them

but when they never showed up
demanding them back,
I helped myself.

*

To keep this secret
I need to be a key.

A skeleton key
with an intricate bit,
a decorative flourish
at the bow.

The sort of key
Mr Rochester used
to lock his wife away.

He will need
to keep me close

if I'm not to open
on the truths
dancing in his attic.

I imagine the first time
Mr Rochester turned his key
and placed it in the pocket
of his riding jacket.

*

When I was a Puritan
I would wake early,
run up a mountain
at the gym,
then select today's
high-necked LBD.
I was my own corset.

Alcohol never passed
my lips and my liver sang
from banned hymnals.

In restaurants, studying the menu
for any hint of animal,
I coughed on the smoke
of my friends' relationships,
thanking God that a ten-hour
workday quashed the desire
to swipe right.

At night I slept
the full eight hours
of the heavily principled.

He arrived on a jet
from the New World
with a carbon footprint
as big as my apartment.
My capotain blew from my head
down the runway. I don't believe
I even tried to catch it.

*

And lo it came to pass
that he left his spare
phone charger
plugged into the socket
above my bed

and by this sign
I understood
his feelings ran deep
and he would return.

*

You rub out your previous picture
with a sweep of your hand, my favourite part
of this new game, and I imagine you tracing
on the backs of your children, Clearwater Beach,
the sun starting to set, you trying to keep
the one who's had enough entertained.
I like thinking about you being a good father
but I'm trying not to think about your index finger
drawing diagrams on the skin of another woman.
Here come twelve dots in a circle and I realise
this is the Houses of Parliament you're rendering
at gone midnight in my city, and there are all
the landmarks of London still to be drawn.

*

I like to travel back to significant moments
in your life. The first dance
at your wedding, though I daren't
turn the sound on and hear what music
is playing, I'm pretty certain
it's a Springsteen song. The birth
of your eldest daughter, you elated
at the hospital calling your parents –
but hang on, isn't that me, exhausted,
holding the baby, in place of your wife?
Scrap that. Let's go to the scene
where your software company takes off.
I can appear as your dependable
programmer, coding late into the night.
No, I think I'll be a sexy new corporate client,
putting you through hoops for my business.
I go back to your high school prom.
I'm two years old toddling along
the locker-lined corridor. Cut.
I'm seventeen, standing by the punchbowl
watching you kiss Annette, your first
serious girlfriend, secure in the knowledge
that she won't make it beyond your first semester.
Or shall I be seventeen days shy of forty-four,
pulling up alongside you in the parking lot
as you walk Annette to your father's Morris Minor?
An English woman new in town, winding down
my window to ask for directions, desperate
to hear you call me *Sweetheart* as only you can.

*

Until I met you
I didn't have anything
worth stealing.

Now I have a phone
I'm scared to use
in public,

a diamond
on a chain
around my neck.

And you yourself.
In the pub we're all
a little tipsy –

you touch
my friend's arm,
she touches you back.

Jealousy corkscrews
through me,
fizzes away.

I'm so fabulously
bourgeois
these days.

*

He gave me a metaphor,
an initialled heart,
to wear around my throat
while he was 4,000 miles away.

At first I was embarrassed.
Such a blatant display of affection –
so American! Then I wore it
openly for two days.

On the third day after he left
I preened in front of the bathroom mirror,
sent his love spinning off its thread
down the plughole.

I couldn't retrieve it.
Tried chopsticks, a magnet.
Declared myself cursed – so English! –
as if I were in a Hardy novel.

My American phoned. *Baby,*
I'll buy you another.
I wept. Then I called a plumber.
He freed it from the U-bend

where it rested, tangled
in my frosted hair. Said *Is this*
what you're looking for? Placed
my metaphor back in my palm.

*

I take my American boyfriend to Margate
so he can see what it means to be English.
On the hottest day of the year
teenagers outnumber seagulls.
We walk the promenade holding hands
and the topless leader of a group of lads
asks my boyfriend *Where are the birds?*
as if he's just found me on the harbour arm.
My boyfriend is unfamiliar with this term
but he gets the gist and we discuss
the American use of chicks but he insists
that went out with the nineteen sixties.
After a round of what I call minigolf
but he calls putt putt I change
into my swimsuit in the Patrons Only toilet,
which he calls bathroom and shudders
when we English refer to the sanitary hardware.
I brave a dip in the North Sea
while he sits on a rock in his sneakers.
He's adamant we reapply my sunscreen
though by now it's well after five o'clock.
Now it's time for supper. He is not
at all familiar with the English rule
that if you see a queue for a fish and chip shop
you join it, nor does he agree that these
are worth the thirty-minute wait.

On the train home he tells me it's impossible
to mess up fish and chips; that if you fry anything
and smother it with salt it's going to taste great.
I disagree, as I do with his declaration
that day trips should not exceed eight hours.

*

He takes me on a cruise ship
with a twenty-four-hour buffet.
In the hot tub we learn
that a basketball legend
has gone down in his helicopter
and the bruised neck of the maid
and out-of-court settlement
are not to be tweeted.
Mabel, our maid, shapes
our towels into a swan
and lays it on the bed
while we're at dinner.
With a shake of my hand
I destroy her.

*

My feet walk sand
in and out of water.
You hold my hand,
my shoes in your other.

I'll keep this for the winter.

*

Just before lockdown
he gave me a view.
Do you miss him, City?

Flights were grounded
and he couldn't reach me,
caught between his old life

and the new. Was it greed
or fear that made us call
two countries home?

At night, without his arms
to hold me, I go to sleep
with the blinds open.

But I am not alone.
My phone could flash
at any moment.

The skyline is made up
of smartphones. I find
his UK device, his US.

I pick out every phone
he's owned since we met.
The river is full but calm.

City, I can see you
listening. Speak up.
Where do we go from here?

*

On his left bicep
he had a mole shaped
like a Greek island.
Not Evia,
my grandfather's island,
which is long and thin,
more like Kefalonia.
I loved to cover it
with the tip of my finger.

On our daily video calls
I might suddenly see it
depending on his T-shirt.
I would miss him

more than ever
in that moment,
reach for it on the screen,
hope I wouldn't
cut him off.

He returned when Evia
was on fire and it was gone.
The skin doctor
had burned the mole away.
All that remained
were three spots of land,
the rest was submerged,
nothing much left
for me to touch.

*

Putting on glasses to read and write
feels like meeting in Manhattan,
unable to shake the feeling
I'm walking through a movie.

On and off and on and off:
the words, your face, the words, your face.
Now when we're apart I appear
bespectacled on our tiny screens.

How to make this off/on manoeuvre
when we're together?
I'm Winona Ryder cast
for the first time as middle-aged.

*

Not a ring on my finger.
He gave me braces for my teeth.

I swear my mother thought
I would soon be leaving her

going with him across the Atlantic
to join the citizenship of perfect smiles.

The horror of my five-year-old niece
at an Airbnb in Athens, Greece,

when she finally noticed. *Does it hurt?*
Do other people have them?

Some young people, I tell her.
You're not young, she replies.

Our final night, a restaurant
looking out at the sunset, my nephew,

still too little for words, points
at my mouth, gets me to grin, guffaws.

Yes, I'm a menopausal woman
in love like a teenager.

And should he abandon me, look,
now my smile is dating-app ready.

There was pain, but I've forgotten.

*

The plane bobs like a cork in waves
two-thirds of the way to Florida
and my stomach starts to protest –
I never grew sea legs or lived up to my name.

What would they make, our Irish
great-great-grandmothers, of this monumental
back and forth, how casually you catch
your flight to London every few weeks

to be with me. I try to imagine boarding
a boat to America assuming I'd never return,
could a sister or mother afford to be spared
to wave a handkerchief from the dock?

Border control: I answer the officer's
questions on how much cash I'm carrying,
how long I plan to stay, pale and desperate
for food like my ancestors before me.

Ancestry.com

The hours I spend
logged on
trying to build

this family tree
this woodland
of my dead

branches tapping
against the window
filling this room

lost children
that didn't reach
the next decade

a great-great-
grandmother banished
to an asylum

names and places –
Rathmullan, Donegal,
Durand, Michigan –

making plans
to visit when just
a county or two

from this laptop
my nieces and nephews
grow another

centimetre
since we were
together.

Childless Married Sisters Are Not to Be Trusted

They'll help you out of a tight spot,
take on your illegitimate baby,
pass it off as their own until the day

the miracle of pregnancy strikes them
and here's a three-year-old
returned to you and your new husband.

Or they'll come to support you
in your hour of need – your husband dying,
five children to take care of –

but really they're eyeing up the kids
for themselves and at your lowest point
they'll make their proposal

and your quietest most amenable daughter
will be removed from the emigrant adventure
on a boat back home

and you'll never see her again.
No, the childless sisters in my family
are not to be trusted. Look at me –

childless sister, childless aunt
snooping around in our grandmothers' pasts
finding fuel for my little stories.

Grandma in London

That is what we called you from the suburb of my childhood.
I did not inherit your exterior but got saddled with your shyness
and in some respects my life has been a disaster.
You were a good-looking woman, a fact that is still remarked
upon in Ireland by your nephews. Even in the nursing home
your fine figure and remarkable cheekbones prevailed.
There was something of the Maureen O'Hara about you,
and like Maureen you entered the film industry, directing Dubliners
to their seats by torchlight. I believe all the movies you watched
on a loop during Hollywood's Golden Age inflamed an overactive
imagination, filling your head with romantic plotlines.
I too love the cinema with its beautiful heroines
pretending to be plain by putting on a pair of spectacles.
Hence, your glasses would never grace your profile in public.

Your attempts at being an upstanding member of the community
did not fool us, your grandchildren. You tickled and rhymed for us
like nobody before or since, and we adored you for it. You played
the mouth organ like we were at a campfire in the Wild West
and John Wayne was about to start singing. You would not rest
until I had mastered my heart's desire, the roller skates, pulling me
around my parents' back garden for hours at a time. I have no use
for this skill in early middle age, but when I skated through Hyde Park
at your side, my head adorned with Deeley Boppers, sparkling red
boxing gloves in honour of Jimmy Cagney, we were sensational.

I have met your secret children, fathers unknown. We have blamed
the Blitz; if you're not sure you will survive the night
you must take whatever comfort you can get. We pray to God
you were fully consenting in this. When my father announced
one Sunday lunch that he had a half-brother (as if we were living
in an episode of your beloved *Dallas*) I assumed he belonged
to my grandfather, your only husband, seeing as he was a sailor
and could have had a woman in every port; but the son was yours,
you who spoke of Anne-Marie, your niece's illegitimate daughter,
so disapprovingly. My father died not knowing he had a half-sister.

I would like to say how proud you would have been
of your eleven grandchildren and fifteen great-grandchildren;
that was not your style, instead you were impressed by everybody else
but never your own offspring. On my recent trip to Kerry,
to get in touch with my roots, I discovered that elevating the neighbours
was rife in your hometown lest one's own family get above itself,
so I am better able to forgive you for not giving us the credit
we deserved. Your adopted daughter was a teacher, and in another life,
one in which penniless orphans received a secondary education,
you might have been a teacher; sometimes I would phone you
for help with my spelling, you were our human dictionary.

This brings me to books. Along with the celluloid of your youth,
your passion was words printed on paper and I find myself
employed as a librarian, like James Stewart's unfortunate wife in
It's a Wonderful Life had she never met him, locking up the library

when everybody else has gone home (but I write words of my own
on my days off). You loved a good novel, as did my father, as do I,
but not the newspapers, cutting out any upsetting articles before
your sons could read them. I myself am trying, in the second half
of my life, to face, head on, uncomfortable realities. Books and films
have been my joy, as has London, which you made your own,
and if I have been undone by our shyness, see how smoothly
I can navigate our city by never meeting anybody's eye.

The City

after Cavafy

I didn't say it out loud but sometimes I imagined
I went to a different country, a different port.
I felt I belonged in a finer city.
I applied for jobs, carefully filled out forms,
but the dream died and now my heart's buried deep
in decay and the flowers of my mind wilt.
Whichever direction I go in, I bump into
the blackened folly of my life, the walls
no longer able to hold up the For Sale sign.

You knew how it was. I'd cross the sea
and land in the same place, my city inside me.
I'd trudge identical streets, in the same poor
neighbourhood I'd get old, watching my hair
turn grey in a mirror that came with the flat.
There's no ship coming to rescue me,
no road out of here. The way I've wrecked
my life in the corner of this rented room,
it's visible from space.

Nursing Home

Cared for by women with no time for vanity,
did you think you were back in the convent?
Dressed in colours you wouldn't have been caught
dead in, Grandma, your undyed hair came
back into its own, a thick white flame.
Was it the medication, your secrets,
or were you finally overwhelmed by diffidence,
but you never spoke a word to me, no recognition.

My visits were like that tale you used to tell
while you worked at some chore you'd found
in my mother's kitchen; the day in the orphanage
when you came into contact with the older girls,
Nell pointing, *See herself, that's Katie, our sister*;
how before that moment you'd no idea she existed.

The Resurrection, Tarbert

Cousin Christie asks me to confirm
some talk he recollects, that my grandfather
was buried at sea. Now that I have toured

the graveyards of Ballylongford, recited
the family names chiselled into the stones,
I share his unease. I used to believe

in cremation, scatter me, maybe, close to my
rented flat on the anonymous grass of Blackheath.
Standing in the graveyard of St Mary's, Tarbert,

relations lying two or three in every row,
for the first time in my life I would have sworn
I was home. If we do rise, Stanley Spencer style,

heaving the lids off of our tombs, blinking
in the perfect light, our naked feet ecstatic
on the green green grass, I would put money aside

to have my body transported here from a far city,
as my great-aunt and uncle have done.
But my grandmother is not here.

She is lost like my grandfather, ashes in a Garden
of Remembrance in Croydon, and it would not
be the same without her to make the introductions.

Inventory

On Facebook I have 484 friends.
I am related to 16 of them.
I have met 41 of them many times.
I meet 79 of them regularly.
142 of them I have met a few times.
89 of them I have met once.
114 of them I have never met.
I haven't the faintest idea who 3 of them are.
I went to school or university with 16 of them.
Around 60 I met in group activities.
Around 270 I am friends with because we share a career.
I would say that 7 of my Facebook friends are best friends.
I would say that 20 of them are very good friends.
Some of my best and very good friends are not on Facebook.
On my birthday 62 of my 484 friends wished me a happy birthday.
This was a reduction of 16 on last year.
This past year I have posted 68 times
on average 5.6 times a month.
I post most frequently when I am on holiday or on excursions
usually holding a glass of fizzy wine.
I am jealous of how often some friends go on holiday,
drink cocktails at the top of tall buildings or have career success,
but to counteract this I click 'Like'
and then I feel better about myself.
I log on to Facebook between 3 and 7 times a day.

Sometimes I am overwhelmed by the sadness
people I hardly know are sharing.
I do not share my sadnesses on Facebook.
I have cried with despair in front of 4 of my Facebook friends.

The Eagle

Could it have been more proud
on Commercial Road with its fresh
plum coat (bless you Historic
Plymouth Inns), a portrait of HMS *Eagle*

painted on its wall, sailing into a sun
which glints behind the roof in the photo
I sent, standing outside its permanently
closed door, to my brother and mum.

Should I be horrified that James Gallagher,
my Irish great-great-grandfather,
after his exemplary career in the Marines,
made his living here as a landlord,

that his son Joseph, my great-grandfather,
showed up in the 1911 census
as a brewery clerk, when my own father
drank himself to an early death?

Never one for social drinking, my dad
rarely set foot inside a public house,
so I'll think instead of the rooms above
bars where I've shared my poems,

of the publicans who make space
for the musicians and poets
and ask us for nothing except
an audience to buy a few rounds;

and I want to believe that my great-
great-grandfather would be no different,
that there'd be a corner in his tavern
reserved for the likes of me.

American Dream

I meet more great-grandparents, English on both sides,
in the Ellis Island Registry Hall. Is that a surprise?

Look, they're making it through the health check.
There are no farms hiring them now in Kent

and they're tired of being dirt poor so the Goodings
have come to America (a good English name that nobody

will ask them to change). Albert, my great-grandfather,
three of his siblings, both parents and his girlfriend,

my great-grandmother Alice Ramsbottom, whose misspelt
surname will make my computer search difficult

(perhaps she was too scared to correct the entry clerk
but she's run away with Albert and wants to part

with it anyway). They won't linger in New York; a farm
in Michigan is where they're headed. It's going to be hard

in the Midwest at the start of the twentieth century.
In eight years Alice will be widowed, lose half her children

to relatives and local families needing labour; my grandma
Dorothy will find herself back in England, aged six, with her aunt.

But the car industry is steadily driving towards Dorothy's siblings and their descendants. That's another story.

I imagine the relief of Albert and Alice at having arrived and passed the test. I smile and have my photo taken.

In the red tiles beneath my feet is their reflection, queuing joyful and tiny beneath the vaulted ceiling.

Fairytale of New York

The only Christmas song I can listen to
any day of the year, and when I do,
I think about my father and the tin whistle
he bought me one half-birthday
from the music shop near his office.

During the worst of The Troubles
my grandma tried not to speak out loud
in London so strangers wouldn't hear
her accent. But this song, when the accordion,
banjo, drum and cittern kick in,

marked a turning point for my family,
led to the leprechaun magnet with the words
It's great to be Irish! across his green belly,
picked up by my dad at Dublin airport,
to live on the fridge during my teenage years.

I could have been someone. Well so
could anyone. It got him, gets me, every time.
Will they stay together? The outro plays,
it's Christmas Eve, and though I never did
I'm waltzing in my father's arms.

Les Parapluies de Cherbourg

My uncle lies on the roof
of the youth hostel in Athens
because all the rooms are full.

He cannot sleep. It is not just the heat
or his grief at the death of his father
whose family he has come to find

but the singing, in French,
from the open-air cinema;
Catherine Deneuve in a raincoat,

her heart breaking, night after night,
But I'll never be able to live
without you . . . Don't go. I will die.

It is 1964. My uncle is 21.
No need to sleep, dear Uncle,
hum along, count the stars.

There is separation and rain
and a remembrance. I open it again
like an umbrella.

Neró

I would say, does this not explain my love of prawns,
as I order the fish platter at the restaurant
selling the freshest seafood as recommended
by my cousin's husband, except weren't vol-au-vents
the first to go from the buffet table
of every English party I've ever been to?
And I would say, as my uncle points out the shell
of a warehouse across the road, which flooded,
destroying all the goods my great-grandfather
had stored there, ruining his business, well obviously
that explains my fear of losing everything, of it all
going belly up, but isn't that the universal fear?
My father, who could barely swim, loved to float
on his back, his belly protruding proudly from the ocean
towards the empty sky, I think he would appreciate
the Greek habit of simply standing in your sunhat
up to your neck in water. And I would say, clearly,
the view from the church where my grandfather
was baptised explains my love of a tree-lined mountain
above a bay of turquoise sea, but doesn't everybody
love a coastline viewed from altitude and surely the most
urban heart can appreciate the symmetry of the cypress?
However, the precarious family homes that you reach
at an angle of ninety degrees, that get snowed in some winters,
I think they might explain why my siblings and I believe
in our legs as the finest form of transportation.
I would grant myself that as inherited.

Certainly this place is imprinted in my bones
but if it wasn't for this blue and white paper table cloth
depicting a map of the island, laid on for holidaymakers,
I couldn't pinpoint where I was and I'm as incongruous
as this orange metallic jug sparking sunlight
and right now the Greek word for water escapes me.

The Required Amount Has Been Reached

The resolute voice
of the ticket machine
follows us on the tram
to the beach

and she is my niece

twenty years from now
switching effortlessly
Greek to English
England to Greece.

If They Should Find Themselves

My Irish relatives
   know by heart
my grandparents' long-vacated
   address, where to head
if they should find themselves
   in London.

Do elderly cousins
   in Greece
declare now and then
   the name of that street
in accented English?

   Hereford Road
you shall be
   my ancestral home.

Where a Greek sailor
   fell in love
with an Irish waitress
   to the tune
of an air-raid siren

   and where
you came from
   and where
you were going
   was by-the-by

you were here and alive.

Little Anchor

for Sofia at two weeks

Tattooed to our sister,
little anchor
holding us steady.

Setting us to work
bailing out
any qualms we have

about the leaky vessel
of family.
Even your uncle,

sceptical pirate,
strokes your cheek
and swears allegiance.

ACKNOWLEDGEMENTS AND NOTES

Acknowledgements are due to the editors of the following publications in which some of these poems have appeared: *Amaryllis, Bad Lilies, Christmas Music: Ten Poems of Comfort and Joy, Jogos Florais, Magma, Nevada Street Poets: a Pamphlet to Celebrate Ten Years, Poetry Ireland Review, Poetry London, The Rialto, Ten Poems About Friendship.*

Some of these poems were published in the chapbook *Anchorage* published by Grey Suit Editions, 2020. Thank you to Anthony Howell and Kerry-Lee Powell.

Earlier versions of 'My Father's Soldiers' and 'A Year Today' were first published in the pamphlet *Bye for Now,* published by The Rialto, 2005. Thank you to Michael Mackmin for his support of my work for over twenty years.

'The City' is a version of a poem by C. P. Cavafy with translation assistance from Nektarios Oraiopoulos.

The epigraph to 'The Glass Jail' is from W. S. Graham's poem 'What is the Language Using Us For?'.

I was inspired to write 'I took my American boyfriend to Margate' after reading Helen Bowell's pamphlet collection *The Barman* (Bad Betty Press, 2022). 'My Grandma Leaves the Orphanage at Glin' owes a debt to Liz Berry's verse novel *The Home Child* (Chatto & Windus, 2023). 'He gave me a metaphor' owes a debt to Chris McCabe's poem 'U-bend', published in his collection *The Triumph of Cancer* (Penned in the Margins, 2018).

Thank you to The Author's Foundation for a grant which enabled me to visit Tarbert in Ireland and Kymi in Greece, the towns my paternal grandparents are from; to Tom and Joan Mulcaire for making me so welcome in Tarbert; and to Scott Cochran for accompanying me on my more recent family research trips and for his love and support. Thanks for love, support and embracing a writer in the family to Mum, Chris, Gemma, Lydia and my uncles John Thalassinos and Paul Gallagher.

Thank you to Pascal O'Loughlin and the Nevada Street Poets for many years of poetry friendship and encouragement, especially Sarah Westcott for advice on an earlier version of this collection. And grateful thanks to my editor Colette Bryce for her close reading and insight and for helping me to shape these poems into a book.